LITERATURE ACTIVITIES

FOR

YOUNG CHILDREN

Art Projects - Skill Building Activities - Plot Summaries

Written by Dianna Sullivan
Illustrated by Nedra Pence

Table Of Contents

ISBN 1-55734-301-2

Teacher Created Materials, Inc.
P. O. Box 1214
Huntington Beach, CA 92649
© *Teacher Created Materials, Inc. 1989*
Made in U. S. A..

Introduction

Literature Activities for Young Children employs a multi-sensory approach to learning based on twelve popular children's books. This book incorporates a variety of activities to meet the needs and learning styles of young children. Many follow-up suggestions are listed and include the following:

(1) Extended Activities

- finger plays
- games, songs, and poems
- creative movement
- field trip suggestions
- choral reading

- jump rope rhymes
- questioning techniques
- gross motor activities
- dramatic play
- show 'n' share ideas

(2) Art Activities

- stencils
- puzzles
- fingerpainting
- mosaics
- salt dough

- sponge/bleach/candle paintings
- paint blowing
- piñata
- wax crayon rubbings
- tissue overlays

(3) Seatwork

- mazes
- counting
- matching sets to numerals
- sequencing
- categorizing

- hidden pictures
- rhyming
- dot to dot
- tracing
- upper and lower case letters

Special Note:

Because some art projects in this book may present too much coloring for young children, the following options may be helpful.

- Outline the character.
- Color only certain items, e.g. the hat and shoes; specify which colors to use.
- Duplicate pattern pieces onto colored construction paper.
- Have children work as a group to complete one project.
- Glue fabric scraps, paper, glitter, beans, etc. to decorate a project.

Blueberries for Sal

by Robert McCloskey

SUMMARY

On one side of Blueberry Hill Little Sal and her mother are picking blueberries, while on the other side of the hill Little Bear and his mother are eating berries. Both Sal and Little Bear get separated from their mothers. When they try to find their mothers, they get mixed up and follow the wrong mom! Finally, the mothers are reunited with their babies and they start the journey down the hill to their own homes.

SUGGESTED ACTIVITIES

Hold a Berry Tasting Party!   Enlist parent volunteers to supply fresh berries, berry jams or jellies, berry juices and nectars, and berry baked goods.   With the children, discuss which products they like best and least. Record their responses on a class graph. Compare and contrast the different kinds of berries. Explore how they are alike and how they are different. Find out how the different berries grow (on bushes, vines, etc.).

Make a Pail Weaving Project. Make a pail out of tagboard (use pattern on page 9). Laminate for extra durability. Use a one-hole punch to make holes along the outside of the pail. Have the children weave colored yarn or a shoestring through the holes.

Go Berry Picking! Make your own pails out of margarine cups. Punch a hole on each side of a margarine cup. Thread brightly colored craft yarn through the holes and knot at each end to make a handle. Then go berry picking with the class.   Place construction paper berries in various areas of the room and retell the story as the children follow behind you. Let them pick berries as they go. End with a taste of fresh berries for everyone.

Make a Berry Collage. Have the children look in magazines, food ads, and newspapers for pictures of berries and berry products. Cut them out and glue to construction paper or tagboard.

How Many Berries?

1. Count the berries in the pail.

2. Write the number under the pail.

3. Color.

_____

_____

_____

_____

_____

Blueberry Maze

1. Help the child find the berries.

2. Color the picture.

Let's Go Berry Picking

1. Color the berries on the next page.

2. Cut out.

3. Paste onto the pail.

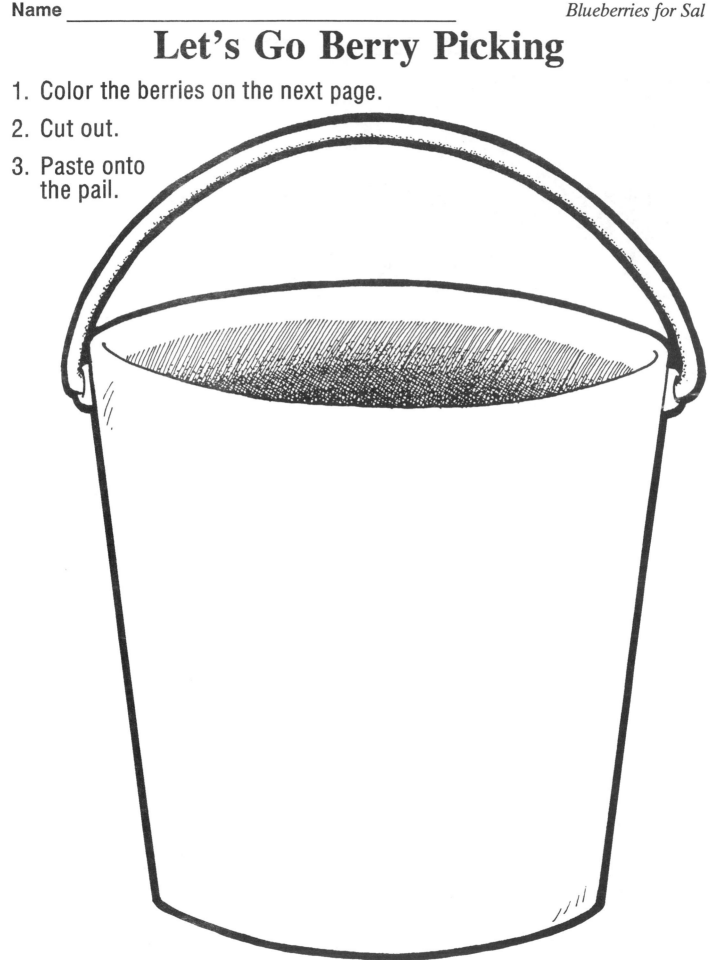

Let's Eat Berries!

Name _____

Hidden Pictures

1. Find the hidden pictures.
2. Circle and color the picture.

pail	t-shirt	bird
spoon	shoe	pie

Pail Pattern

* See suggested activity page 3.

The Very Hungry Caterpillar

by Eric Carle

SUMMARY

An egg on a leaf grows into a caterpillar. The caterpillar eats a variety of foods Monday through Sunday. He is finally a very big caterpillar and is no longer hungry. The caterpillar then builds himself a cocoon. After two weeks a beautiful butterfly emerges from the cocoon.

SUGGESTED ACTIVITIES

Sponge-Paint Butterflies: Body: Supply each child with a 3" tagboard circle. The child traces the tagboard circle onto a variety of colors of construction paper. The child then cuts out the circles and glues them together in one long length. Decorate the end circle with a face. Add antennae out of black construction paper. Sponge-paint the colored circles of the caterpillar's body. **Wing**: Sponge-paint a half sheet of colored tissue paper. Let dry. Fold the tissue paper back and forth into a "fan." Cut off each of the end edges of the fan at an angle. Tie a piece of string around the center of the tissue paper "fan". Spread the "fan" out on both sides. Tape or glue the wings behind the "butterfly body."

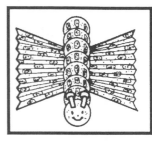

Observing Caterpillars: Place some real caterpillars in a jar for a day or two for classroom observation. Provide caterpillar information, magazine pictures, books, etc. for future classroom study of caterpillars.

"What The Caterpillar Ate" Memory Game: Each pupil in the class takes turns telling a new Very Hungry Caterpillar story. "He started to look for some food. On Monday he ate one _____. But he was still hungry! On Tuesday he ate two _____. But he was still hungry!" (Go Monday through Sunday, then start over with Monday again. Numbers can go as high as you want.) When all the pupils have had a turn, let the pupils draw everything he/she can remember the caterpillar ate. The pupil that draws the most correctly remembered items wins this memory game!

Nature Items Scavenger Hunt: Divide the pupils into two or three groups. Give each group an identical list of nature items (twig, rock, blade of grass, soil, green leaf, yellow leaf, orange leaf, brown leaf, seed, caterpillar, ant, flower, etc.). The group with the most items on the list wins!

Waxed Nature Collections: Gather small colored leaves, flattened flowers, blades of grass, etc. Place the objects on a sheet of waxed paper in an organized, nicely laid out collection. Place another sheet of wax paper on top of the collection. Iron these objects between the two sheets of wax paper.

The Very Hungry Caterpillar

1. Color and cut out your caterpillar art project pieces pages 11 -14.

2. Glue Tab A to Side A.

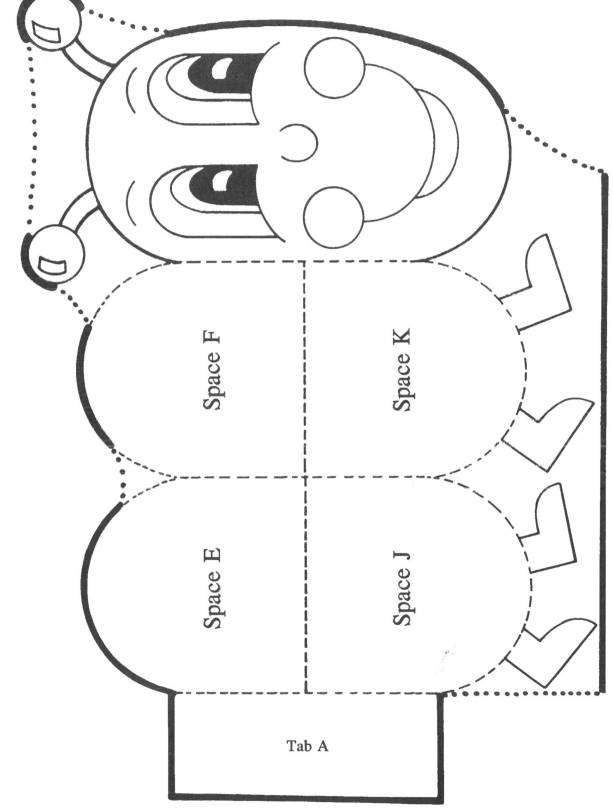

The Very Hungry Caterpillar

Side A

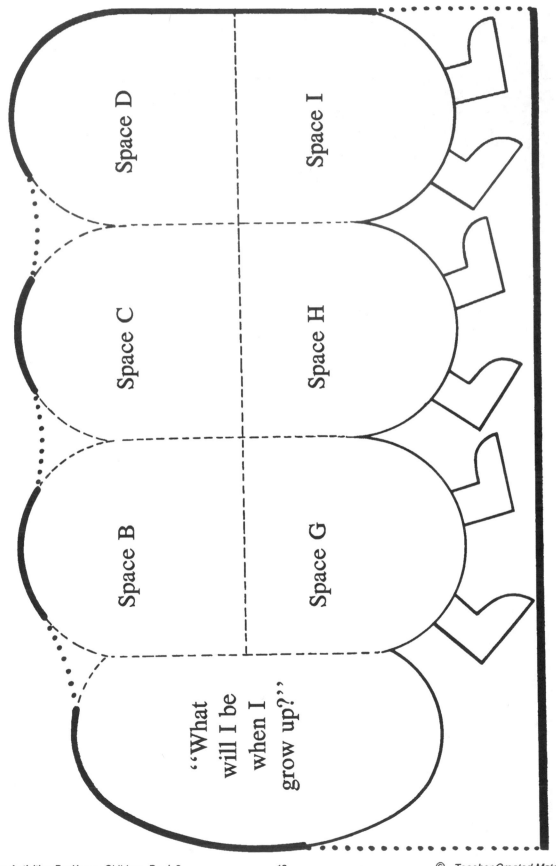

Space D

Space I

Space C

Space H

Space B

Space G

"What will I be when I grow up?"

The Very Hungry Caterpillar

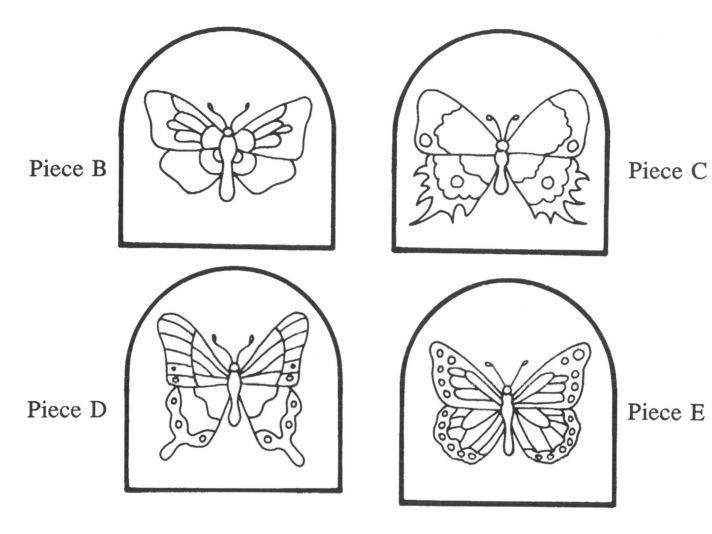

Piece B

Piece C

Piece D

Piece E

Glue pieces B-K onto space B-K on caterpillar.

The Very Hungry Caterpillar

Piece F

 Piece G

Piece H

 Piece I

Piece J

 Piece K

A Butterfly Is Born

Cut out pictures and glue in order.
Color.

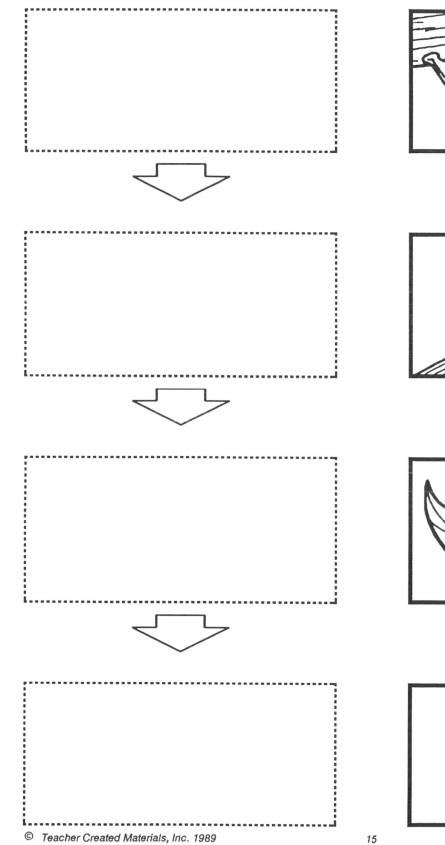

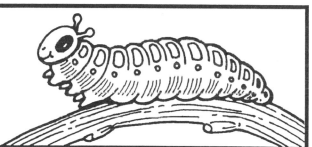

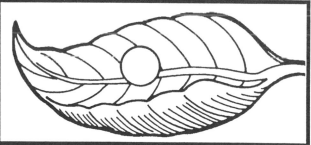

Fruit Number Words And Numbers Booklet

1. Color and cut out booklet pages (pages 16-18).

2. Trace the numbers and number words on each booklet page.

3. Punch out all the holes on each page.

4. Assemble the booklet in numerical order.

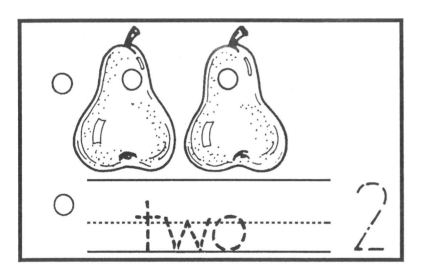

5. Tie the booklet with string or yarn through the left hand side holes.

6. Once the book is completely assembled, you will see uniform holes through all the fruits on each of the pages (Pretend the caterpillar ate through all the fruits!).

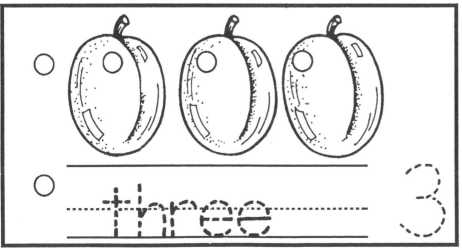

Fruit Number Words And Number Booklet

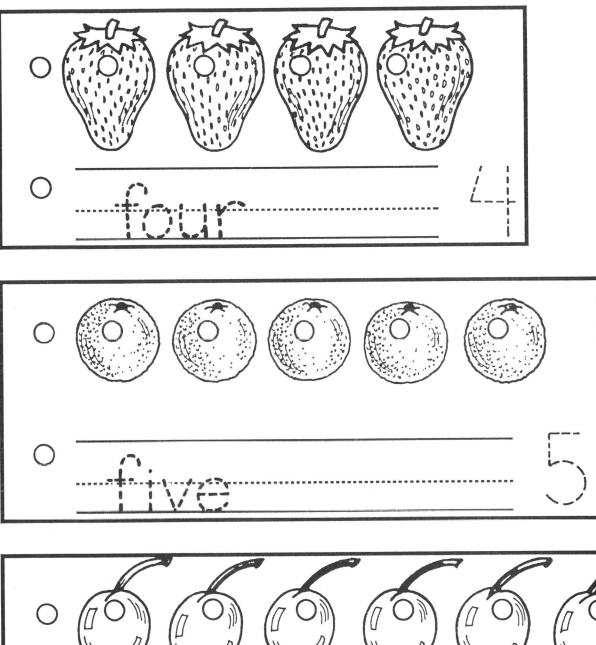

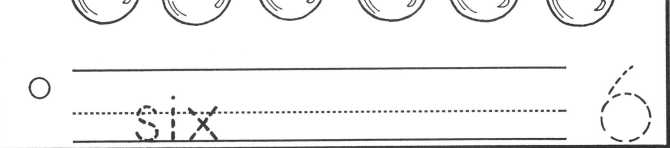

Fruit Number Words And Number Booklet

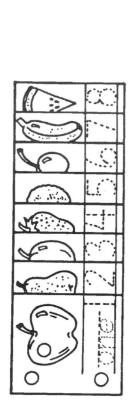

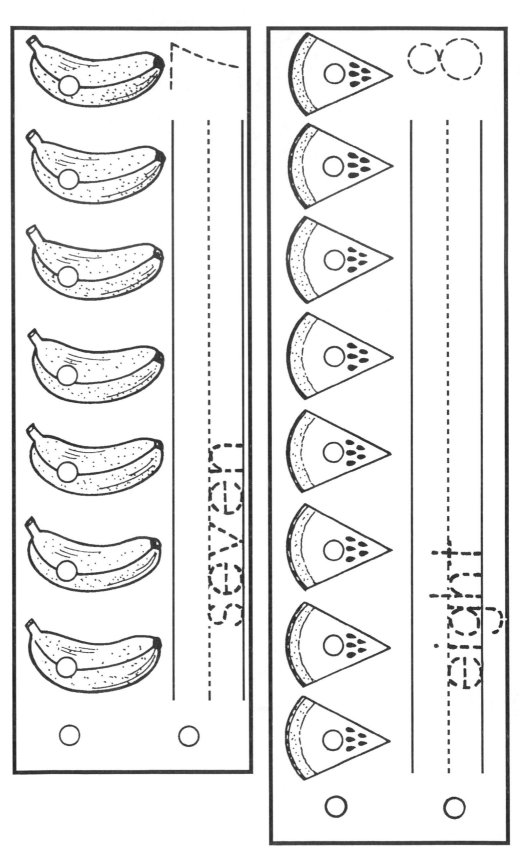

Winnie-the-Pooh

by A. A. Milne

SUMMARY

Pooh's craving for honey leads him into many adventures with his friends. He raids and escapes from a beehive and is stuck for days in a rabbit hole. Pooh gets caught in a wind storm, has an encounter with a tiger, a rain storm and a flood, and has many more adventures.

SUGGESTED ACTIVITIES

Glitter Yarn Bear: Duplicate the bear outline (page 27) onto heavy paper. Cut out the bear shape. With a black marker draw eyes, nose, mouth, paws, inside of ears. Mix one teaspoon of wallpaper paste into a half pint of cold water. Let this mixture stand for fifteen minutes. Soak a long piece of colored yarn in the paste mixture; let the excess paste drip off the yarn. Make a "free" yarn design on the bear. Use many colors of yarn. Sprinkle a variety of colors of glitter onto the wet yarn. Let the bear dry thoroughly, then shake off the excess glitter.

Bear Beans Mosaic: Duplicate the bear outline (pages 27) onto white construction paper. Glue the white construction paper bear to a piece of colored tagboard. Collect some beans (e.g. kidney, coffee, lima, navy, and split peas, rice, barley, etc.). Apply glue thickly and heavily with your paint brush to a small portion of your mosaic. The glue dries quickly, so do only a small portion at a time. (White household glue or wallpaper glue works well.) Glue the beans onto the paper in an organized, nicely arranged mosaic. For the "mosaic look", leave a very small space between each bean you glue down. Completely cover the bear with mostly brown beans. Cover completely the background paper with split peas, rice, barley, etc., separating the brown bear from the background color.

My Bear

1. Draw a face on your bear.

2. Color and cut out bear on pages 20-23.

3. Punch out holes A-E.

4. Attach bear's arms and legs to bear's body by inserting paper fasteners through holes A-E. Be sure to match like letters.

My Bear

My Bear

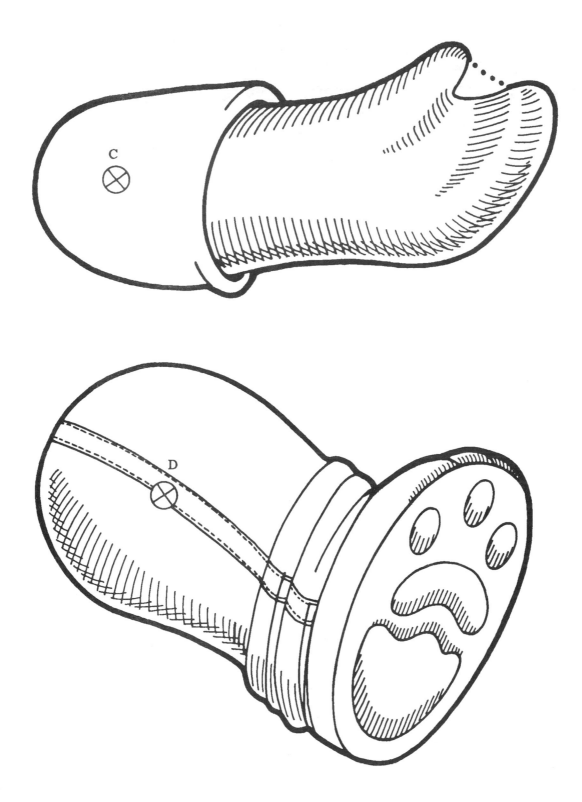

My Bear

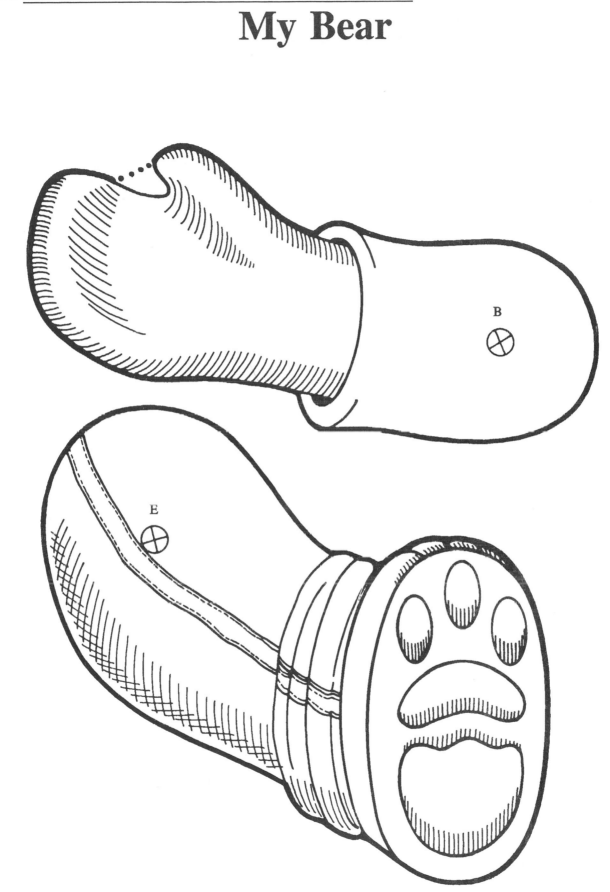

Rabbit Hole

Help the bear find his way out of the rabbit hole.

How Many Bees?

1. Count the bees.   3. Color.
2. Write the number.

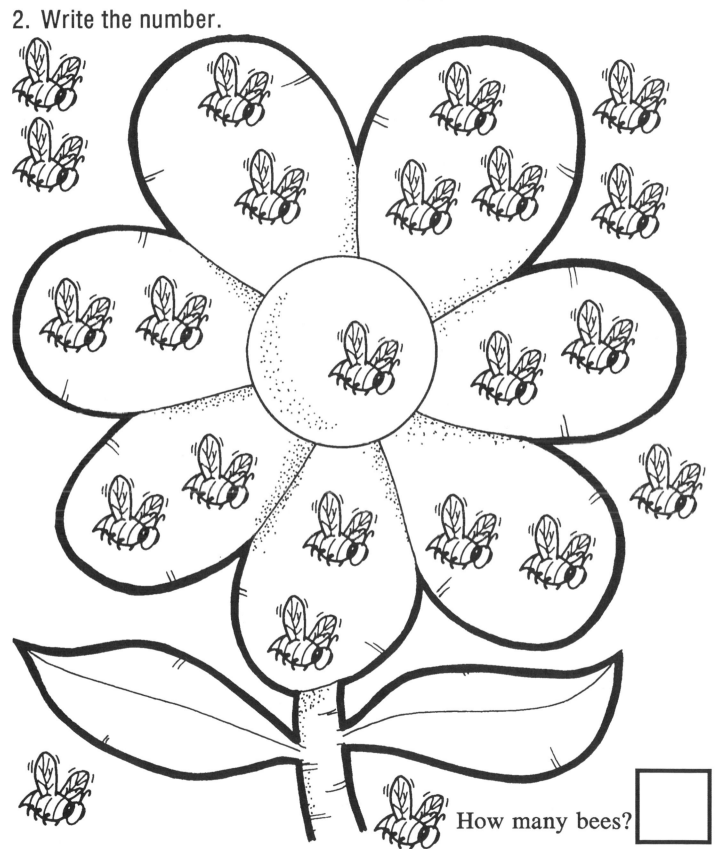

How many bees?

Animal Friends

Color, cut and paste to complete the characters.

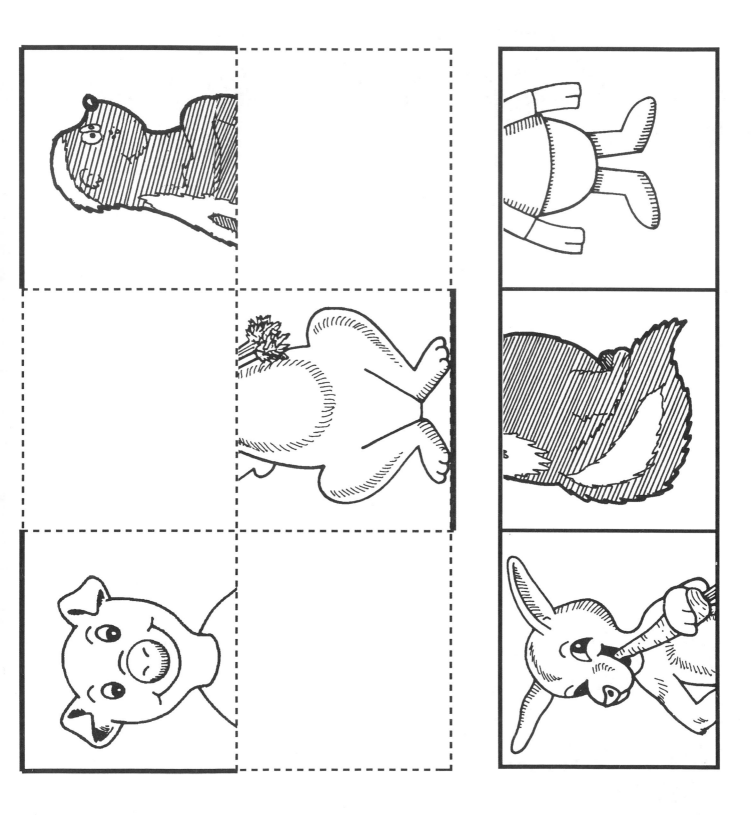

Bear Pattern

* See suggested activities
page 19.

Green Eggs And Ham

by Dr. Seuss

SUMMARY

Sam tries to get his friend to eat some green eggs and ham. Sam's friend does not believe he would like green eggs and ham and refuses to eat them. Sam is very persistent and tries to get his friend to eat the eggs and ham in his home and outside of his home. They both have many adventures as Sam's friend tries to escape from eating the green eggs and ham. Finally Sam's friend tires of trying to escape Sam. He tastes the green eggs and ham and discovers he likes them!

SUGGESTED ACTIVITIES

Glued Yarn Eggs: Cut an egg shape out of colored tagboard or poster board. Child draws a simple glue design on the egg and then places pieces of colored yarn on top of the glue.

Yarn Eggs: Cut out an egg shape from tagboard or poster board. With your hole punch, punch out several holes all over the egg. Using a darning or tapestry needle threaded with a long strand of yarn, make creative designs all over your egg. Several yarn colors will add to your egg.

Punch Dot Eggs: Cut out an egg shape from colored construction paper. With your hole punch, punch out several holes all over the egg. Glue this egg onto a contrasting color of construction paper. The holes are now the contrasting color! Cut around the egg shape. Another variation would be to glue a variety of colors behind the punched out holes, glue tissue or cellophane paper behind the punched out holes. Overlapping of colors always produces an interesting project.

Cross-Stitched Eggs: Cut an egg shape out of 1" graph paper. With a darning or tapestry needle threaded with yarn, make a cross-stitch in some of the squares. glue the cross-stitched egg onto a colored piece of construction paper. Cut around the egg shape.

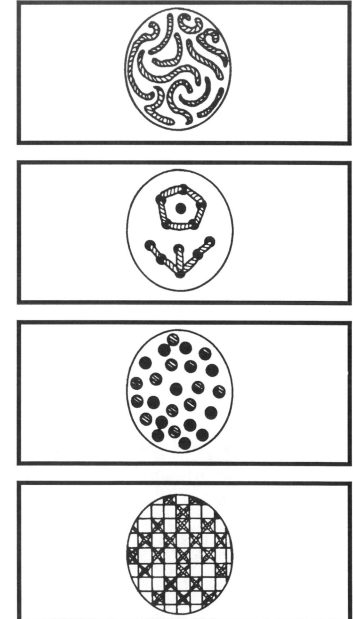

Dinosaur Delight

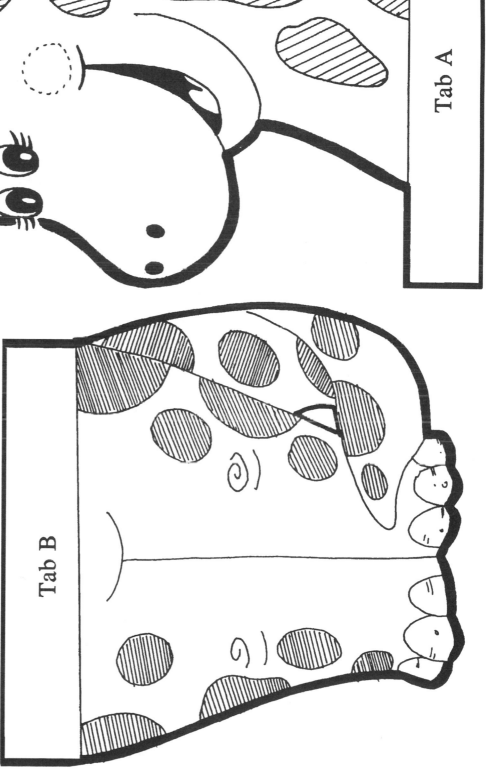

1. Color and cut out dinosaur on pages 29-31.

2. Glue dinosaur's head, Tab A, to top of book.

3. Glue dinosaur's legs, Tab B, to bottom of book.

Dinosaur Delight

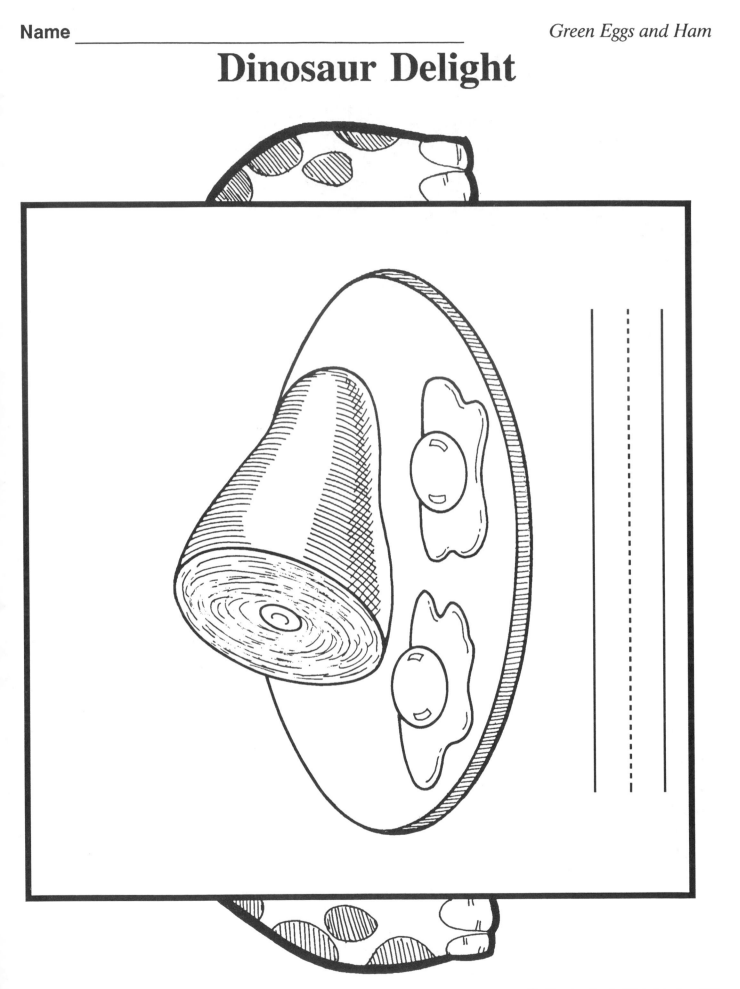

Dinosaur Delight

Duplicate this page 4 or 5 times for each pupil and then on the left hand side, staple the pages on top of the art project character's page. Pupil writes one color word on each page and colors the ham and eggs that color. The character then holds a color word book.

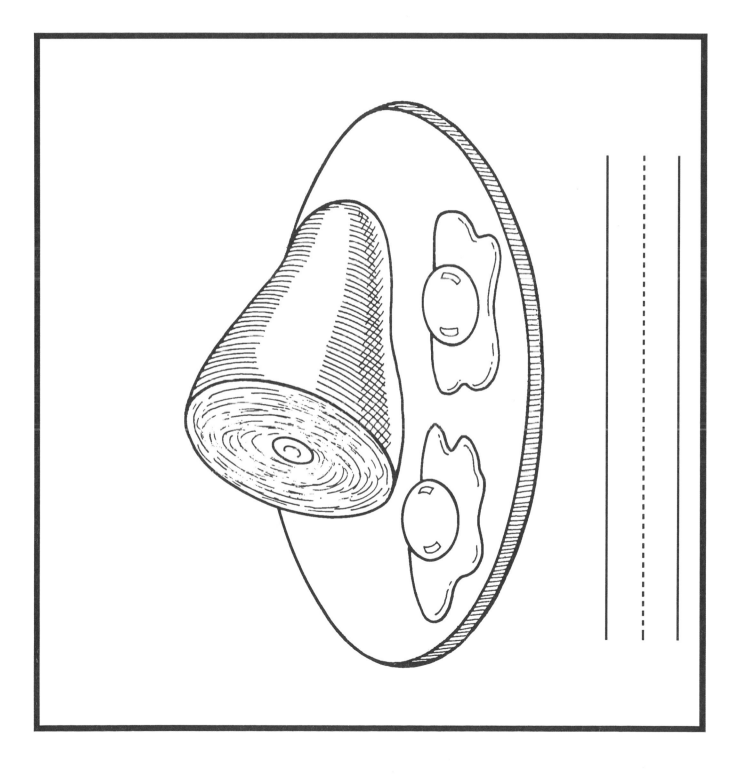

"I Do Not Like . . ."

1. Find the hidden message.
2. Match the lettered eggs to the number blanks below.

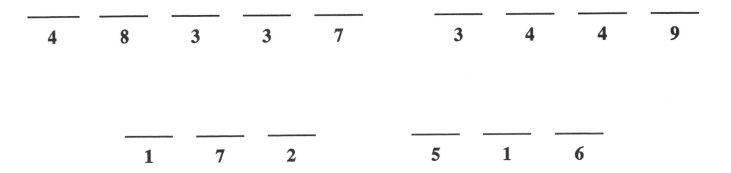

____ ____ ____ ____ ____   ____ ____ ____ ____
 4   8   3   3   7   3   4   4   9

____ ____ ____   ____ ____ ____
 1   7   2   5   1   6

Find My Rhyming Pair

1. Find the two things that rhyme.
2. Color them the same color.

Name _____

Green Eggs And Ham

* See suggested activities page 28.

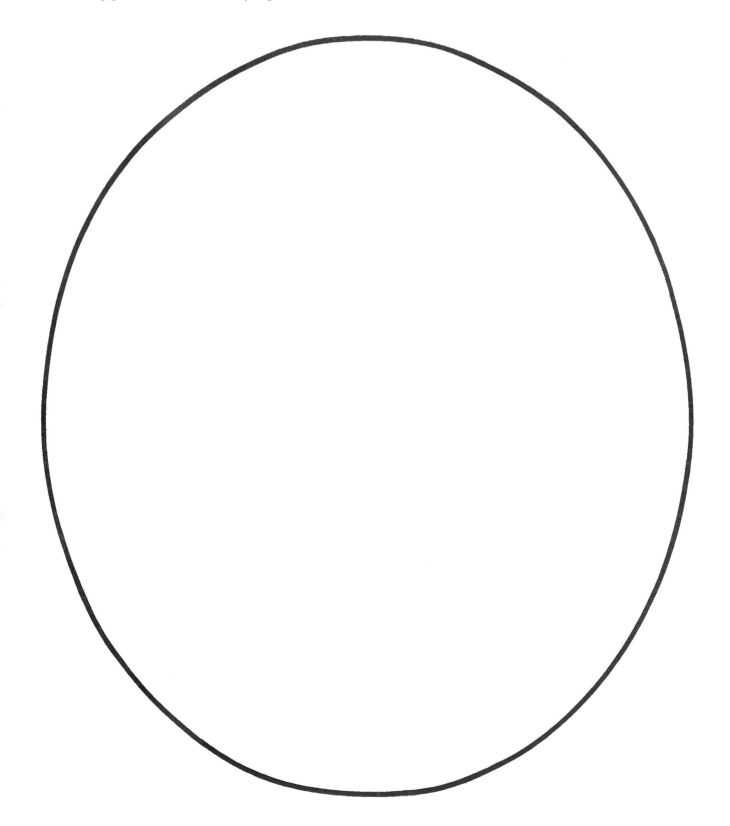

Clifford's Birthday Party

by Norman Bridwell

SUMMARY

Clifford's people family and the children in the neighborhood throw a birthday party for Clifford. They celebrate Clifford's birthday with food, a pinata and lots of birthday presents. Clifford received his best birthday gift at the end of the party. His dog family pops out of a pretend birthday cake! Clifford's favorite birthday gift is having his family and friends at his birthday party.

SUGGESTED ACTIVITIES

Clifford's Birthday Gift: Each child decorates a small paper bag at home (e.g. crayons, paint, colored markers, construction paper, glitter, etc.). He/she puts a birthday gift for a dog into his/her sack (e.g. bone, dog food, toy, leash - items can be real, drawn, or magazine pictures). During a show-and-share time, the child gives the other classmates "clues" or "hints" about his/her dog gift. The other classmates guess the gift the child has brought for Clifford.

Clifford Mask: Spray paint a large paper plate red. Let dry. Cut out some dog ears out of red construction paper (see patterns on page 37). Glue the ears onto the plate. With your black marker or crayon, draw a nose, mouth, and eye holes. Cut out the eye holes. Glue a tongue depressor to the bottom of the plate.

Crayon Painted Birthday Presents: Keep all your crayon colors separate. Peel the paper off the crayons. Grate the crayons on a cheese grater creating crayon shavings. Put the shavings into a small can. Add a small amount of turpentine to the shavings in the can. Mix until smooth like paint. Copy the gifts (page 41) onto white construction paper. Cut the gifts out and paint them with your crayon paints. Let them dry thoroughly. Glue the gifts to a colored piece of construction paper. Add a ribbon bow to each package.

Party Dog

1. Put a face on your party dog.

2. Color and cut out the dog on pages 36-38.

3. Glue dog's back end (page 38) to Tab A.

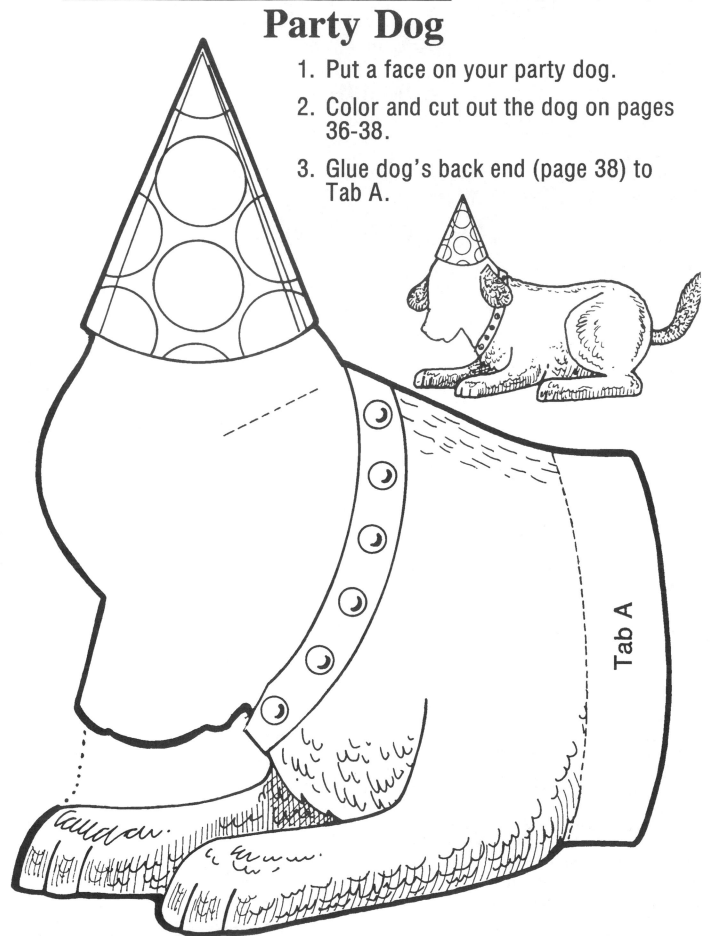

Tab A

Party Dog (Cont.)

1. Glue the dog's left ear behind the left side of his face.

2. Slip and glue right ear in slit on dog's face.

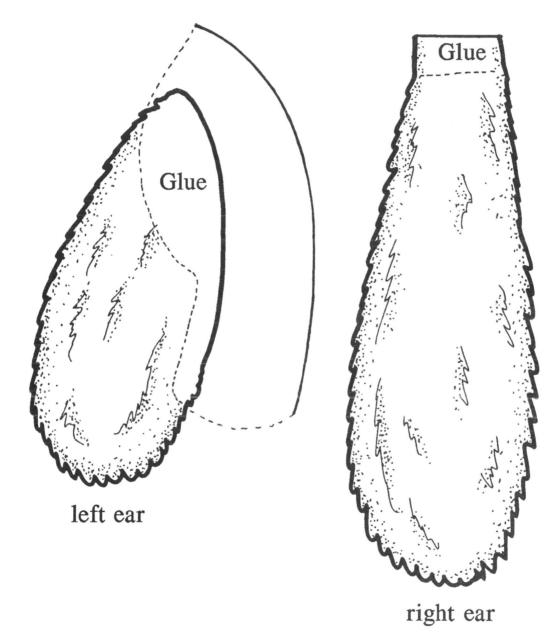

left ear

right ear

* See suggested activity page 35.

Party Dog (Cont.)

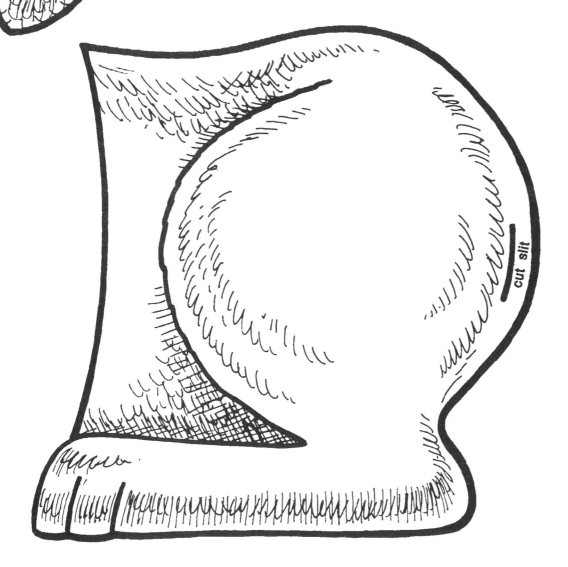

Tail: Fold Tabs B and C under. Push the tail piece into the straight line on dog's back end. Flatten out Tabs B and C. The tail moves back and forth slightly.

Name _____

Presents For Clifford

1. Color the presents Clifford got for his birthday.
2. Circle Clifford's best birthday present!

Gift Certificate for Clifford

Name _____

Clifford's Birthday Party

Color by numbers.

1	red	4	green	7	brown
2	yellow	5	orange	8	black
3	blue	6	purple	9	pink

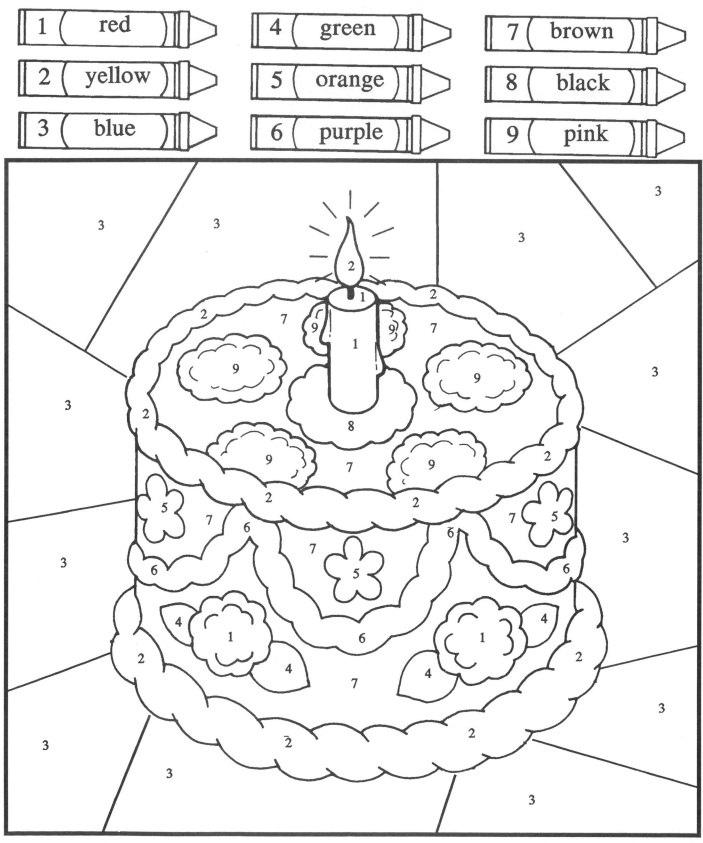

Birthday Presents

* See suggested activity page 35.

The Carrot Seed

by Ruth Krauss

SUMMARY

A little boy plants, weeds and waters a carrot seed. His family does not believe his carrot will grow. The little boy, believing his carrot will grow, waits patiently, continuing to nurture his seed. The little boy succeeds in growing a large carrot.

SUGGESTED ACTIVITIES

Torn Carrot Art Project: Fold a 9" X 12" piece of orange construction paper in half (length-wise) and make a torn carrot. Tear green tissue paper into long strips (approx. 1 inch in width and 6 inches in length). Attach some of the strips to the top part of the carrot. Draw lines on the carrot with your black crayon or marker.

Carrot Crayon Resistant: Color a large carrot on a 9" X 12" piece of white construction paper. Fill the carrot shape in completely with orange crayon and the carrot top with green crayon. Do a brown water color wash over the orange carrot half of the picture and a blue wash over the green carrot top part of the picture. The carrot is now growing beneath and above the earth.

Planting Carrots: Plant carrot seeds in a large jar. Watch your carrot grow!

Carrot Nail and Wood Picture: Make a carrot shape with chalk on a piece of scrap wood. Pound in the nails along the carrot shape. Twist orange yarn around the nails on the lower carrot portion and green yarn around the nails on the top carrot portion.

The Carrot Seed

Wheelbarrow

Color and cut out the girl and wheelbarrow on pages 43-45.

Glue the wheelbarrow handle (by the girl's hand) to Tab A (page 44).

Space D

Tab B

Wheelbarrow (Cont.)

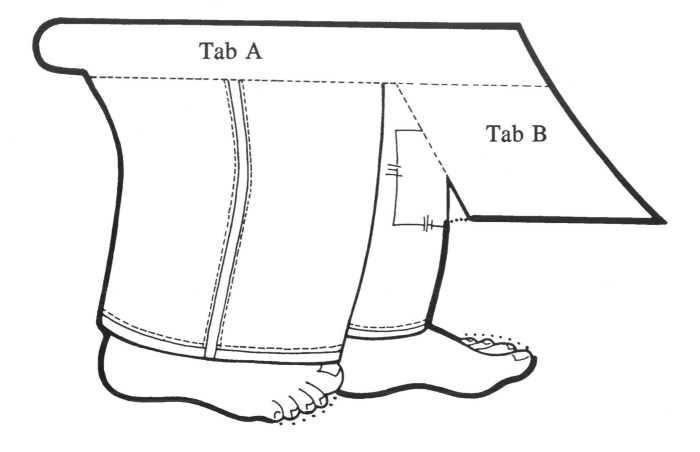

Tab A

Tab B

Wheelbarrow (Cont.)

Attach the wheelbarrow to the girl by gluing Tab C onto Tab B (pages 43 and 44).

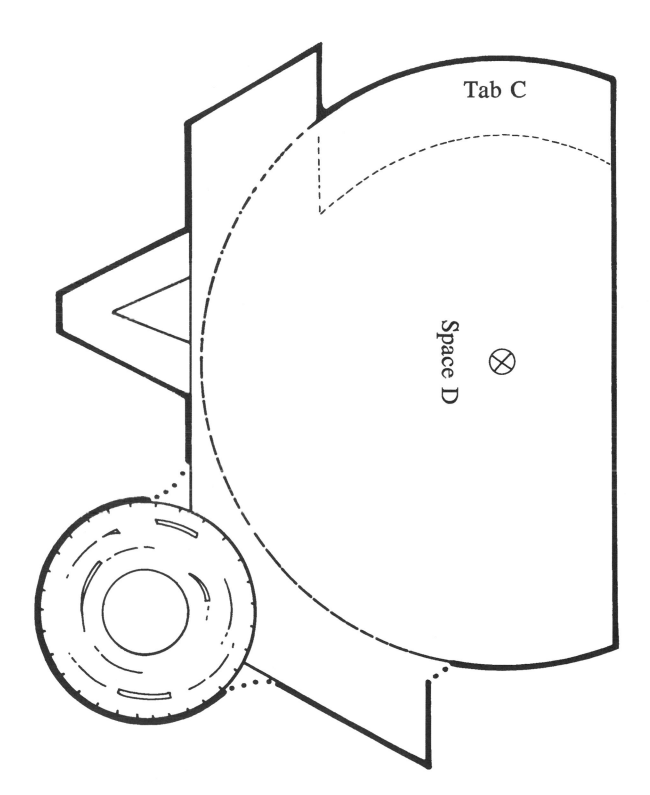

Tab C

Space D $\otimes$

Wheelbarrow (Cont.)

Color and cut out the vegetable circle and glue the circle down onto space D (page 43 and 45).

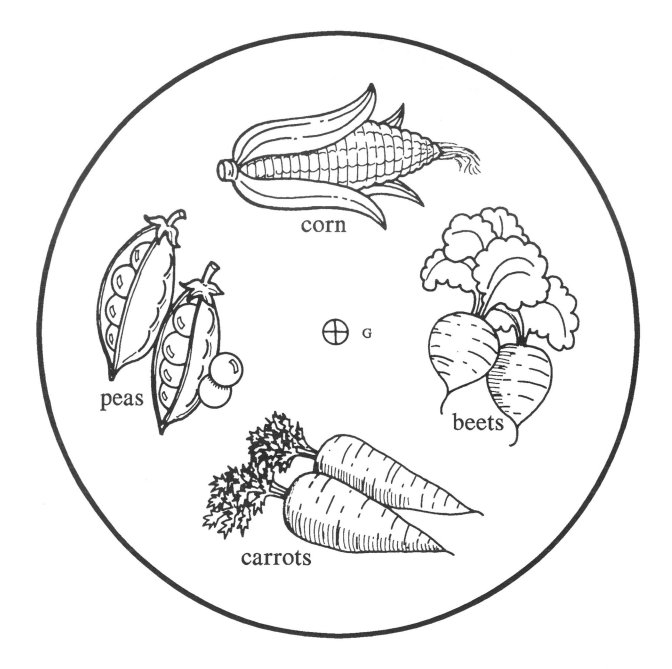

Wheelbarrow (Cont.)

1. Cut out the circle and space E on the circle below.

2. Insert a paper fastener through holes F and then G (pages 46-47).

3. Turn the wheel and name the vegetables.

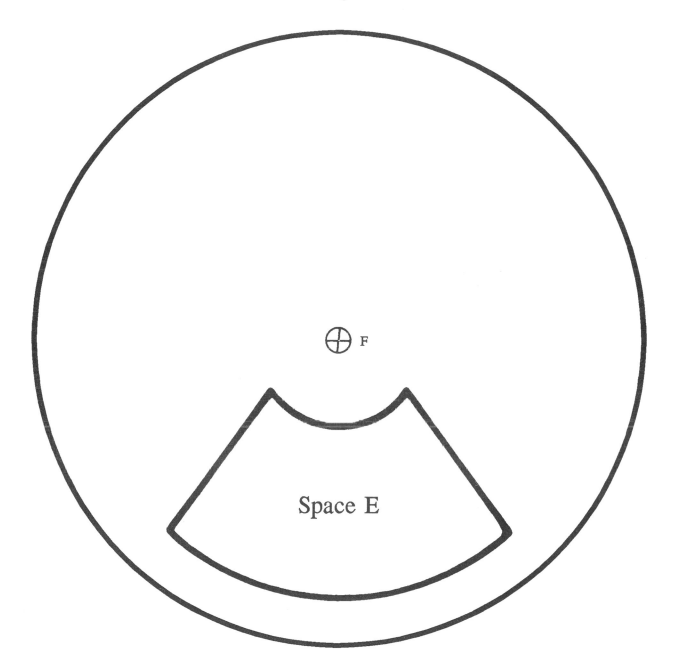

F

Space E

Growing A Carrot

1. Color the pictures.
2. Cut and glue in order.

Carrots Are Vegetables

Connect the dots.

Color.

Mike Mulligan And His Steam Shovel

by Virginia Lee Burton

SUMMARY

Mary Anne the steam shovel is replaced by the new gasoline, electric and diesel shovels. Not needed for city work anymore, Mike Mulligan and Mary Anne go to the country. In the country they dig the cellar for the town's new city hall. Mary Anne is not able to get out of the deep cellar hole that she has just completed digging, so the new town hall is built over her. Mary Anne is then given the new job of being a furnace for the town hall and Mike Mulligan is given a new job as the town hall's janitor.

SUGGESTED ACTIVITIES

Hardware Collage: Collect a lot of nuts, bolts, screws, washers, nails and other small hardware items. With your paintbrush, apply a thick layer of wallpaper or white household glue onto heavy colored tagboard; cover only small portions at a time as the glue dries quickly. Glue the hardware items onto the tagboard in a collage arrangement.

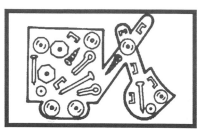

Steam Shovel Creative Movements: Children pretend they are a steam shovel (rolling over the ground, up and down hills, digging up dirt and laying the dirt aside, making canals, roads, airport plane strips, etc.). Make machine sounds.

Machine And Sand Tray: Put some sand in a dish pan. Add some machine toys (trucks, shovels, tractors, etc.). Let the children play!

Machines "Show 'N' Share" And "Free Play": Children bring their toy machines (shovels, cars, trucks, etc.) to school. Each child shows their machine to the other children and shares his/her knowledge about the name of the machine, how the machines works, what job it does for man and whether it works with other machines, etc. Allow 15 minutes of "free play" for the children to explore their machines.

Machine Riddles: Make up "machine riddles." "I'm thinking of a machine that digs holes." "What machine is it?" (steam shovel). Before beginning the riddles, show several machine pictures and discuss what each machine does.

Dig In!

1. Connect the dots.
2. Color the picture.

Gasoline, Electric, Diesel Motor Shovels

Color, cut and glue to complete the shovel.

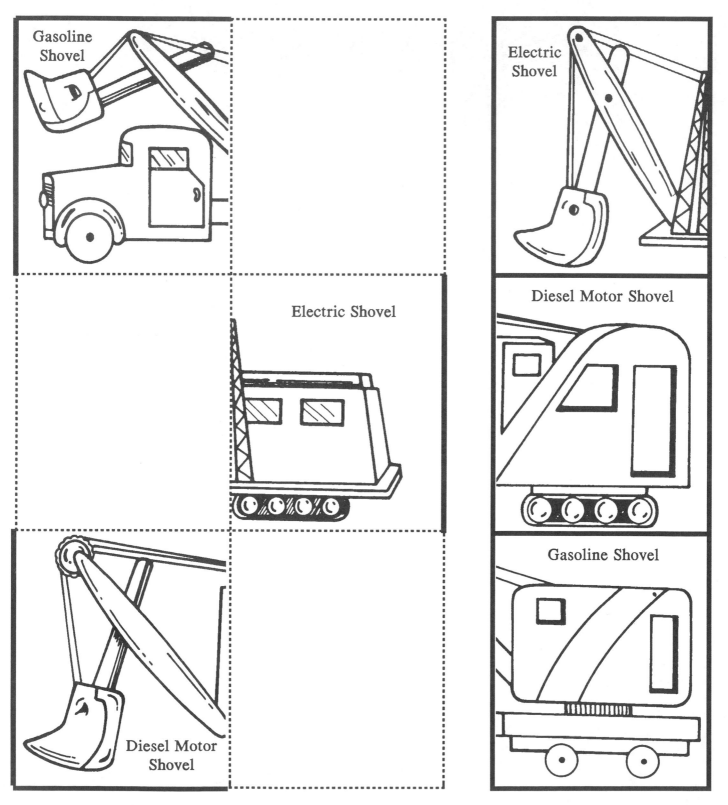

Gasoline Shovel

Electric Shovel

Electric Shovel

Diesel Motor Shovel

Diesel Motor Shovel

Gasoline Shovel

Color Shapes

Color by shape.

Steam Shovel

1. Circle the one that is different in each row.

2. Color the ones that are alike.

SHOVELS

Color and cut out the shovels.

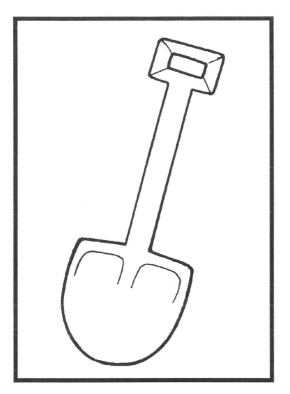

Paste the shovels in order from smallest to largest.

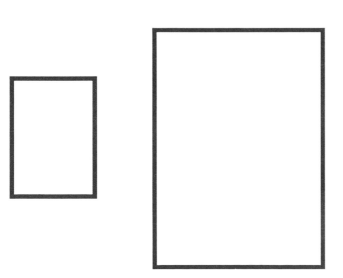

Steam Shovel Pattern

1. Duplicate this pattern onto heavy tagboard and cut out.

2. Apply white glue to a small portion of the steam shovel.

3. Sprinkle with sand.

4. Repeat steps 2 and 3 until the whole steam shovel is covered.

Harry The Dirty Dog

by Gene Zion

SUMMARY

Harry dislikes getting baths. One day he buries the scrub brush and runs away from home. Harry proceeds to have all kinds of adventures that lead him into getting very dirty. He begins to wonder if his people family has noticed he has run away. So he returns home. No one in the family recognizes this dirty, strange dog. Harry does many of his old dog tricks in hopes they might recognize him but they do not. Being unsuccessful, he digs up the scrub brush, runs into the bathroom, and jumps into the bathtub. The family decides to give the strange dog a bath. As they scrub the dog clean, they recognize their pet Harry!

SUGGESTED ACTIVITIES

Dog Paper Mosaic: Duplicate the dog outline (page 64) onto white construction paper. Cut several colors of construction paper into one-inch squares. Keep the squares separated by colors. Glue each square onto the dog. For the "mosaic look," leave a very small space between each piece you glue. Completely cover the dog with mostly one color of squares: brown, yellow, etc., or brown with black spots. Cover completely the background paper with another color to separate the dog from the background.

Flour Paste Dirty Dog: Duplicate the dog outline (page 64) onto white construction paper and cut out. With a black crayon or marker, make a face and spots on the dog. To make the dog dirty, mix some flour and water together into a runny, thick paste. Add some brown tempera paint and mix. Spread the paste completely over the white construction paper dog. With a comb, make swirls, curves and lines into the brown paste. This leaves a dirty "patterned" dog.

"Drop the Handkerchief" Circle and Singing Game: Beall, Pamela and Susan Nipp. *Wee Sing And Play.* California: Price/Stern/Sloan Publishers, Inc., 1986 (page 22).

Rhythmic Movement To Songs: Children can move rhythmically to songs about dogs. Let them feel the music and bend their bodies to the music's moods and rhythms.

Learn About Dogs: Discuss and show pictures whenever possible about: (1) breeds of dogs, (2) dog senses, (3) dog intelligences, (4) useful dogs, (5) dogs as pets, (6) care of dogs (feeding, shelter, grooming, diseases), and (7) training dogs.

Clean Dog . . . Dirty Dog

1. Match the clean dog to the like dirty dog.

2. Color the dogs.

58   © *Teacher Created Materials, Inc. 1989*

Bath Time Puzzle

1. Cut out the pieces.

2. On a sheet of construction paper, glue each piece together to make the picture.

3. Color.

Paw Prints

1. Color the paw whose letter is different.
2. Write the letter that is different in the box.

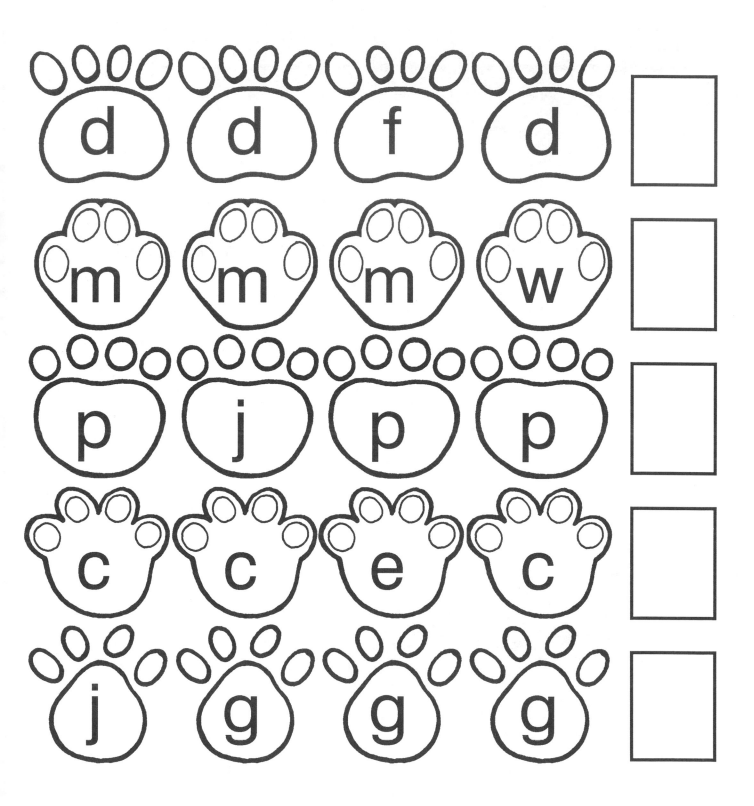

Matching Spots

1. Cut and paste the matching spots on the dog.
2. Color the dog.

Where Is the Dog's Bath?

1. Color the paw prints that lead to the bath tub.
2. Color the picture.

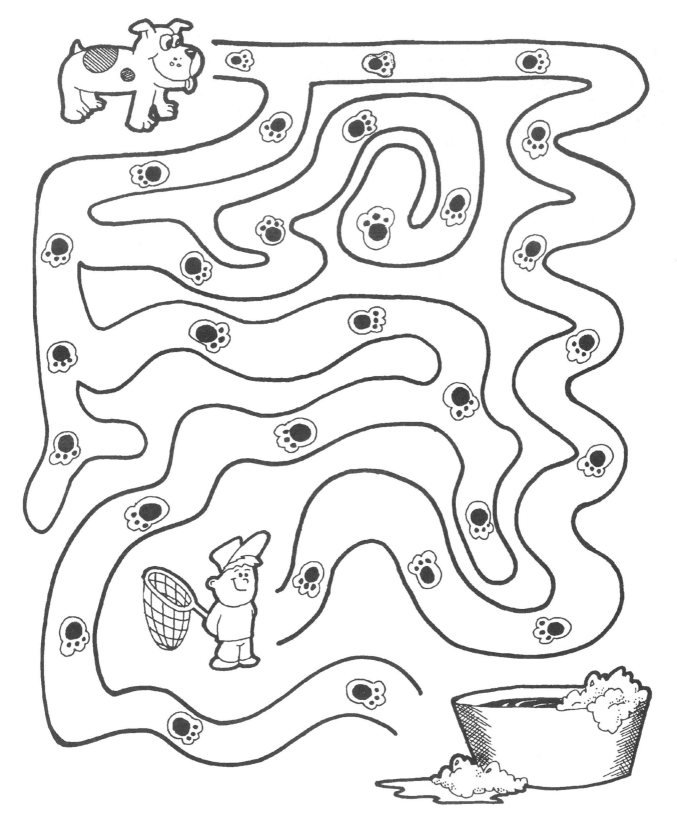

62

Spots

1. Color and cut out.
2. Punch holes.
3. Insert straws.

Name _____

Dog Pattern

* See suggested activity page 57.

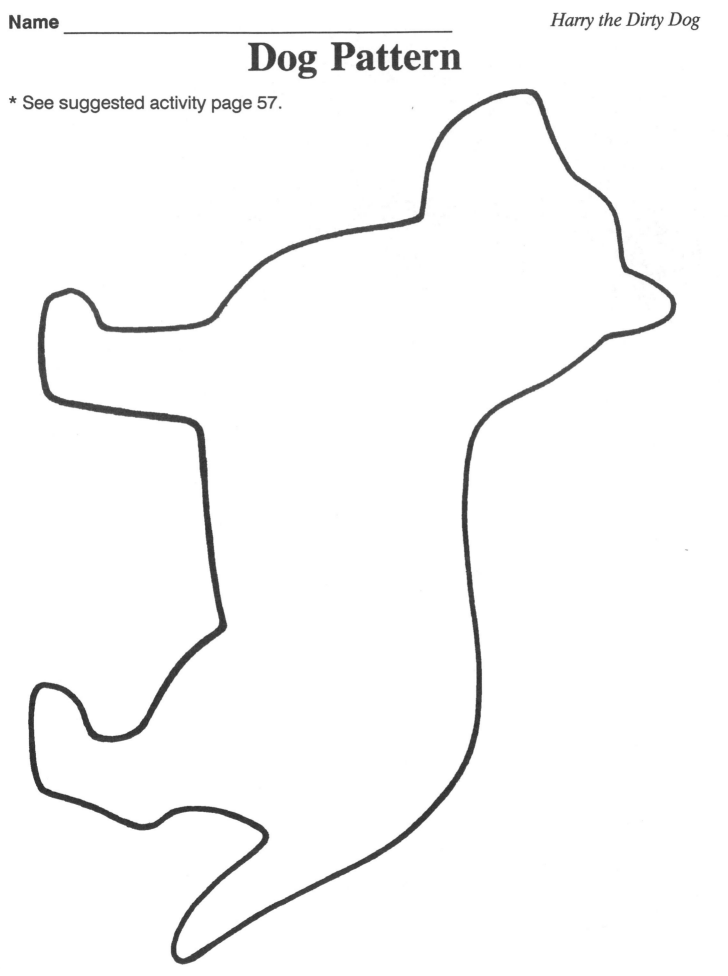

The Snowy Day

by Ezra Jack Keats

SUMMARY

Peter wakes up one morning to discover that it has snowed the night before. He puts on his snowsuit and begins to explore the snow outdoors. He makes footprints and tracks, hits snow off the trees with a stick, watches a snowball fight, makes a snowman and snow angels, and slides down a snowy hill. When it's time to go inside his house, he makes a snowball and puts it inside his pocket so he can look at it the next day. It melts immediately. The next day he arises to see a new snowfall.

SUGGESTED ACTIVITIES

Tempera Paint Snowy Picture: With white tempera paint, paint a "snowy" picture on blue construction paper.

Sponge Paint Snowman: Cut a sponge into small pieces. Dip a piece of sponge into the white paint and "print" the sponge onto a sheet of blue construction paper. Make a snowman (two circle shapes). Dip a piece of sponge into the black paint and make a hat, two coal eyes, a nose, a mouth, and three coal buttons.

Popcorn And Candy Snowman: Duplicate the snowman shape (page 74) onto white construction paper and glue the shape onto a sheet of purple construction paper. Glue popped popcorn onto the snowman. Add lifesaver eyes, gumdrop nose, mouth and buttons. *Optional:* Add a black construction paper hat (pattern on page 74).

"Snowman" Poem: Silverstein, Shel. *Where The Sidewalk Ends.* New York: Harper And Row Publishers, Inc., 1974 (page 65).

Freezing Experiences: Make homemade ice cream or popsicles.

Dressing For Snowy Weather: Provide the children with a box of old clothes, hats, caps, mittens, gloves, scarfs and boots. They can pretend to dress up warmly for a very cold, snowy day.

My Snow Fun Book

1. Draw a face on your snow person.

2. Color and cut out the character on pages 66, 67 and 69.

3. Glue the character's head, Tab A, to the top of the book (page 67).

Tab A

My Snow Fun Book

Snow Page

1. Duplicate this page three or four times for each pupil.

2. Cut out snow pages.

3. Glue or staple to top of Snow Fun Book (page 67).

4. Pupil may write a story beginning ''On a snowy day I like to . . . .''

5. On the other pages, pupil may color pictures of things he/she likes to do in the snow.

My Snow Fun Book

Glue character's feet, Tab B, to bottom of the book (page 67).

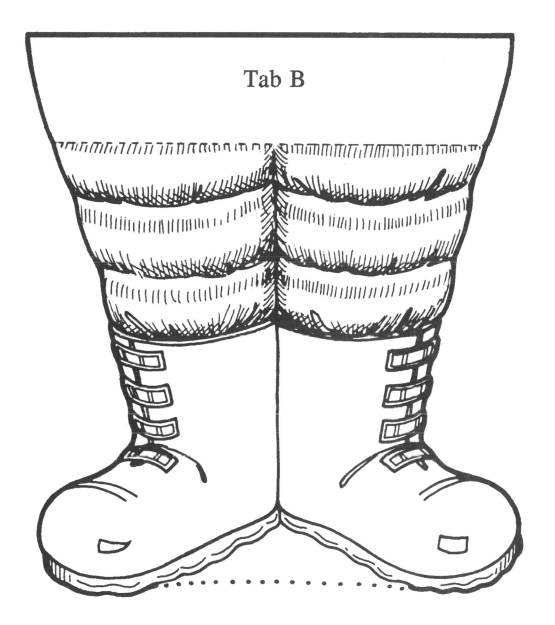

Tab B

Snowflakes

1. Count the snowflakes.

2. Write the number.

3. Color.

How many snowflakes? ▢

Match the Mittens

Cut out the mittens below.

Paste the cut-out mittens next to their letter partners.

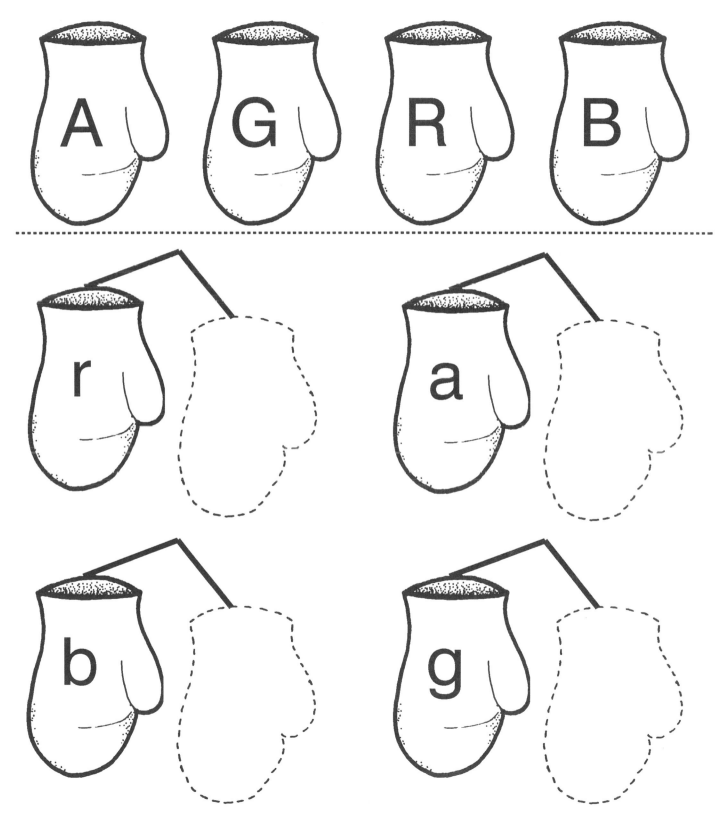

Fun In The Snow

1. Color all the things you can do in the snow.
2. Circle the thing you like to do best.

Winter String Necklace

Color and cut out the rectangles. Fold the rectangles in half along the fold lines. Place a long piece of yarn in between all the folded rectangles. Glue the inside of each rectangle and press the two squares together. Tie necklace yarn ends.

Snowman Pattern

* See suggested activity page 65.

Big Bad Bruce

by Bill Peet

SUMMARY

Big Bruce, the bear, spends his spare time in the forest frightening little animals just for fun. One day he throws a boulder into a berry patch, just missing Roxy, the witch. Bruce thinks this act is very funny. Roxy decides to teach Bruce a lesson. She bakes him a special pie that is cursed with a spell. Bruce eats the pie and begins to shrink. With his new tiny size, the forest animals chase him away. He barely escapes with his life! Roxy takes pity on the tiny bear and takes him into her home. The tiny bear has not learned his lesson. He still continues to scare creatures smaller than himself, this time throwing pebbles at grasshoppers, beetles and caterpillars.

SUGGESTED ACTIVITIES

Rubber Cement Bear: Lightly trace the bear picture (page 81) with a pencil onto a sheet of white typing paper. Cut out the bear. Outline the bear's face with rubber cement (a toothpick or used match stick dipped into the glue are good painting tools.). Next, dip a brush into the glue and make short strokes on the bear's body for a "hairy body" look. Let the glue dry thoroughly. Mix a watery brown tempera paint solution. Paint over the whole bear figure. Let the paint dry thoroughly. With your fingers rub off the rubber cement glue. The face and hair appear white on a brown bear.

Blot Print Bear: Fold a large piece of brown construction paper lengthwise. Have the child trace a tagboard pattern piece of a symmetrical half of a bear onto the fold (pattern on page 81.). Cut out and flatten the bear shape. Drip black paint on one side. Press the sides together and open to reveal a print on both sides of the bear. With your black marker or crayon add a face and paw features.

"The Bear Went Over The Mountain" Song: Beall, Pamela and Susan Nipp. *Wee Sing Silly Songs*. California: Price/Stern/Sloan Publishers, Inc. 1986 (page 29).

"Bear In There" Poem: Silverstein, Shel. *A Light In The Attic*. New York: Harper And Row, Publishers, Inc., 1974 (page 47).

Playing Instruments To Songs: Children beat, shake, rattle, and jingle homemade or commercial instruments to the beat and rhythm of bear songs.

Cookie Dough Bears: Make and then color the cookie dough. Children can make bears out of colored dough.

Bullies: Discuss the following: What is a bully; why some people become bullies; ways of coping with bullies; how a bully can change his/her personality and actions so that he/she is no longer a bully; how to make new friendships without being a bully.

Honey Bear

Color, cut and paste the bees from page 77 onto the hive.

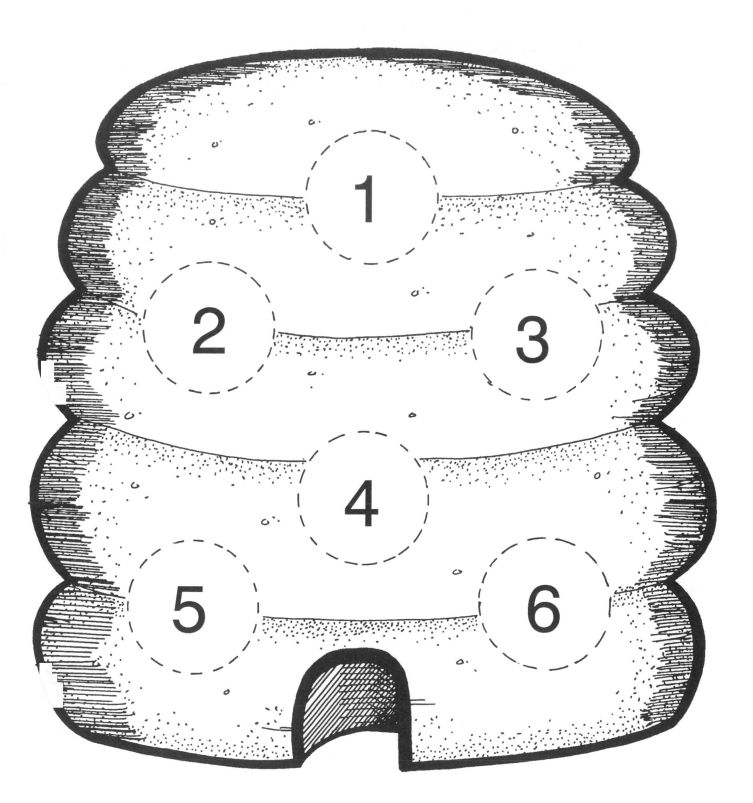

Honey Bear (Cont.)

Big Bad Bruce Matching

Match like big and small pictures. Color.

Forest Animal Book

1. Color and cut out the pictures.

2. Staple the book together.

Name: _____

Where's The Bear?

1. Color and cut out the picture pieces.

2. Glue the pieces in order.

Bear Pattern

* See suggested activity page 75.

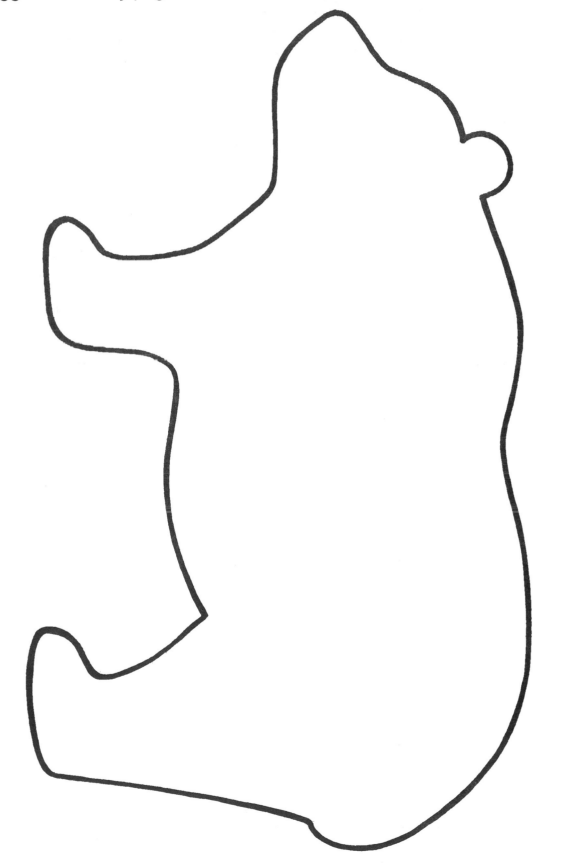

Are You My Mother?

by P. D. Eastman

SUMMARY

A mother bird leaves her nest to look for food before her egg hatches. In her absence from the nest, the baby bird hatches. He immediately begins to look for his mother. He asks several animals and a few machines if they are his mother. One of the machines puts him back into his nest just before his mother returns with some food for her newly hatched baby bird. He is delighted to discover his real mother!

SUGGESTED ACTIVITIES

Bird Seed Mosaic: Duplicate the bird outline (page 89) onto white construction paper. Glue this white construction paper bird to a piece of colored tagboard or heavy cardboard. Collect some seeds (flower, vegetable, bird, popcorn, grass, fruit, etc.). With your paintbrush, apply a heavy coat of wallpaper or white household glue to a small portion of your mosaic at a time since the glue dries quickly. Glue the seeds onto the tagboard into an organized mosaic. For the "mosaic look," leave a very small space between the seeds you glue. Completely cover the bird with mostly one color of seeds. Cover the background completely with another color, to separate the bird from the background.

Stained Glass Bird: Trace the outline of the bird onto waxed paper (page 89). Cut out the bird shape and coat with liquid starch. Layer pieces of blue and orange tissue paper on top of the starch, overlapping many pieces of the tissue paper (creating darker and lighter tones of blue and orange). Let the bird dry. Press the bird with a warm iron to get a stained glass effect.

"Blue Bird" Circle And Singing Game: Beall, Pamela and Susan Nipp. *Wee Sing And Play.* California: Price/Stern/Sloan Publishers, Inc., 1986 (page 26).

"Early Bird" Poem: Silverstein, Shel. *Where The Sidewalk Ends.* New York: Harper And Row, Publishers, Inc., 1974 (page 30).

Dramatic Play: *Characters:* 1 bird, 1 cat, 1 cow, 1 dog, 1 hen. Children can act out the parts of the story where the little bird asks several animals if they are his mother. Each animal answers the little bird.

Match The Nest

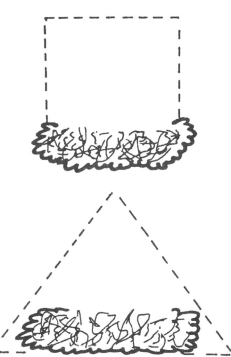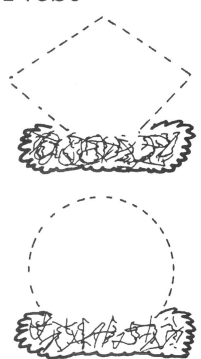

1. Cut out the bird shapes below.

2. Paste them in the correct nest above.

3. Color.

Guess And Draw

1. Connect the dots.
2. Color.

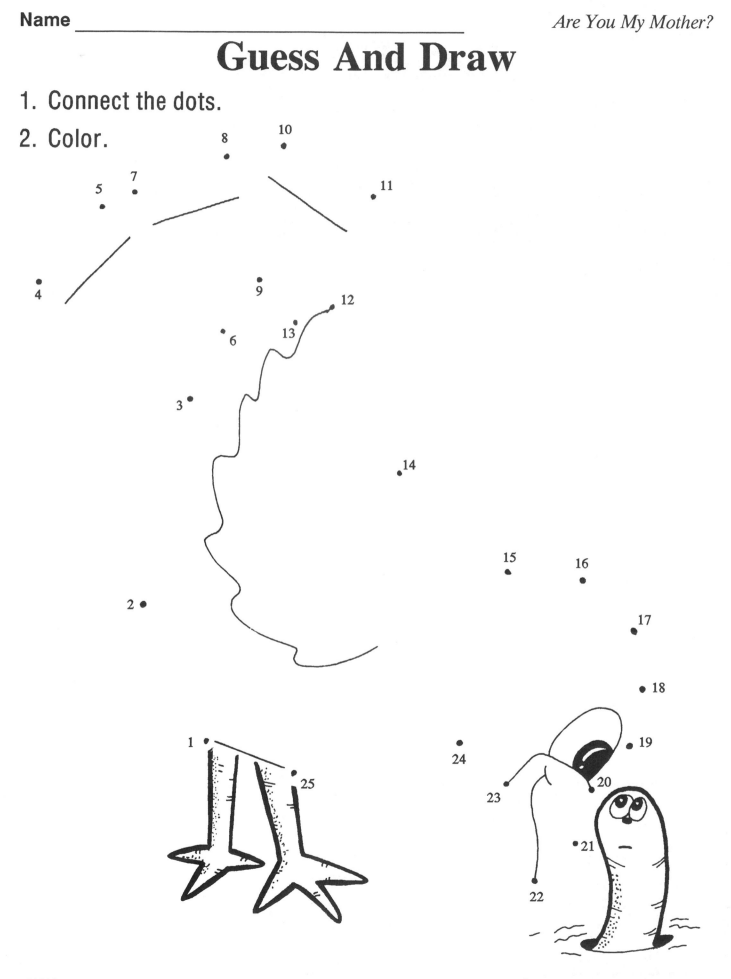

Rhyming Eggs

1. Color nest and eggs below line.

2. Cut out eggs with dashed lines.

3. Glue to rhyming words in nest.

Pretty Bird

Color by number.

| 1 | blue | | 3 | red | | 5 | brown |
| 2 | green | | 4 | yellow | | 6 | orange |

Baby Finds His Mother

Help the little bird find his mother.

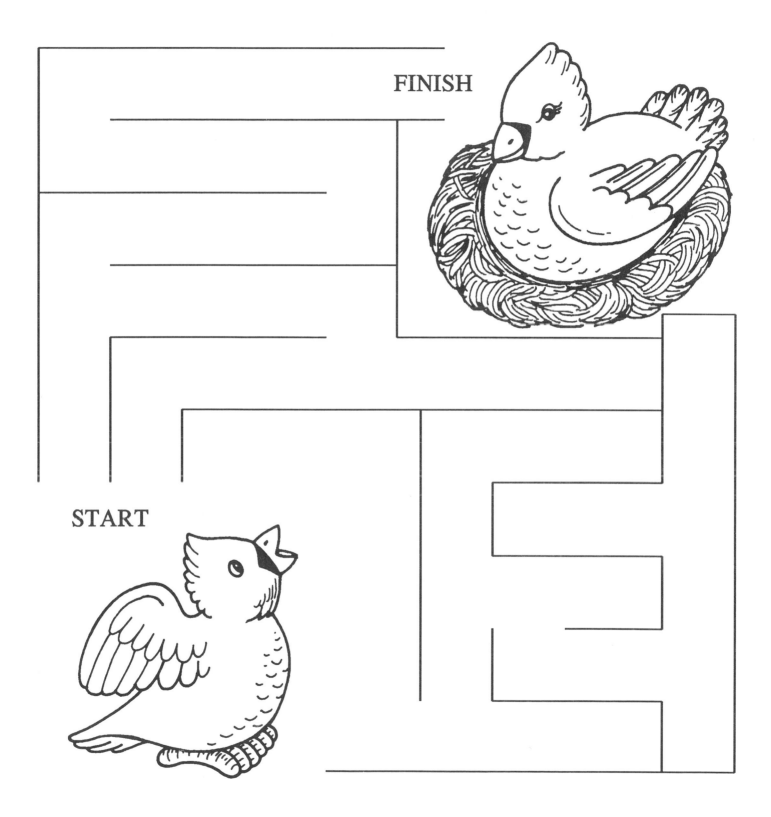

Mothers and Babies

1. Color the mother in each picture.

2. Circle the baby in each picture.

Bird Pattern

* See suggested activity page 82.

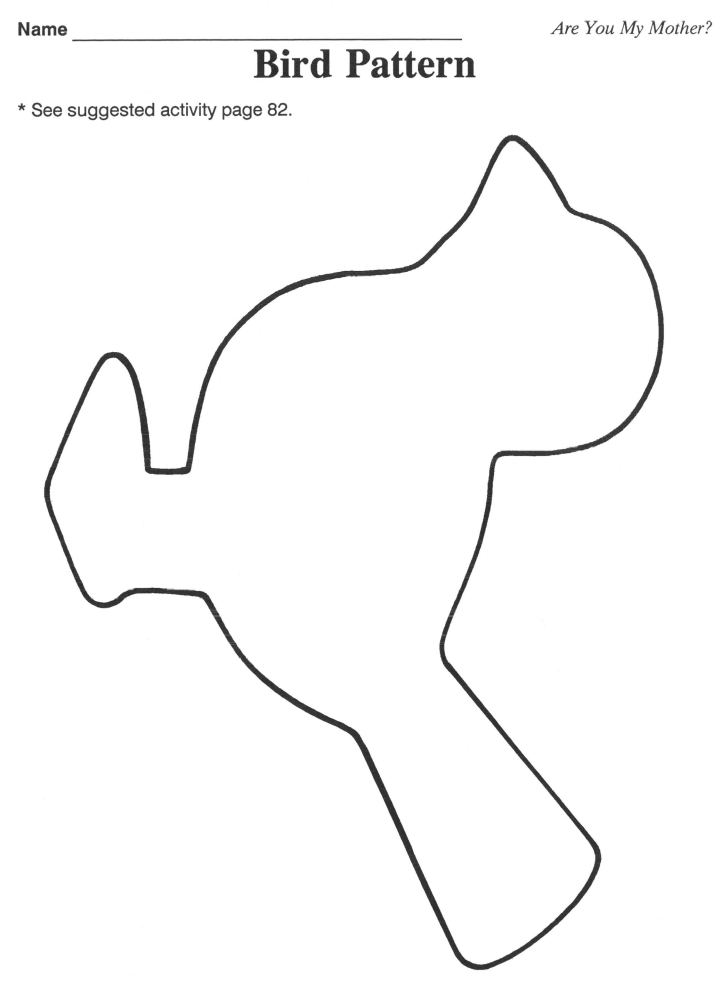

In A People House

by Theo. LeSieg

SUMMARY

A mouse gives a bird a tour of a people house, pointing out the many items in a house. The two make a variety of messes while discovering the uses of the household items. The people in the house discover the mouse, bird and their messes and chase them out of their house.

SUGGESTED ACTIVITIES

A People House: Pupils cut out pictures of objects from magazines, newspapers, or catalogs that could be found in a house (brush, chairs, bed, fork, etc.). Make an outline of a house on tagboard (see pattern on page 96.). Label each room. Glue the object in the proper room.

Pencil, Colored Pencils, Wax Crayon Object Rubbings: Place the flat object on the table. Place a sheet of typing paper over the flat object. With the pencil or crayon, rub over the object. A print of the object will appear on the paper.

Household Items Scavenger Hunt: Divide the pupils into two or three groups. Give each group an identical list of household items (comb, bobby pin, crayon, thimble, yarn, clothes hanger, etc.) Pupils take the lists home. The group collecting the most items on the list wins!

Object Take Away Game: Place some household objects on a table. Have the children cover their eyes. Take away one of the objects. The children guess which object is gone. **Alternative**: *Object Addition Game.* Add an object; children guess which object was added.

Remember The Object Game: Place some household objects on a table. Have the children study the objects on the table for a minute. Cover the objects with towel. Each child takes a turn verbally listing all the objects he/she remembers seeing on the table.

Be A Household Object: Children form their bodies into the shape of the household object. Pretend each object is moved by external force. Have the children imitate:

1. Scissors opening and closing.

2. A popcorn seed popping.

3. A piece of thread going through the eye of a needle.

4. A rollerskate moving over cement.

5. A blanket floating down on top of a bed.

My House Is Nice

1. Color, cut out, and glue the things that can go in a house.

2. Color the house.

Name _____

House Things

Circle and color the things in each group.

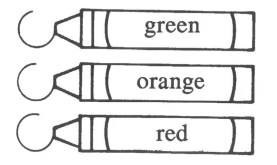 green — things in the kitchen

orange — things in the living room

red — things in the bathroom

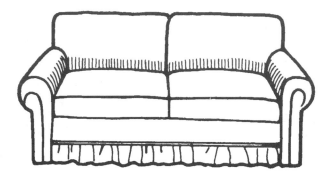

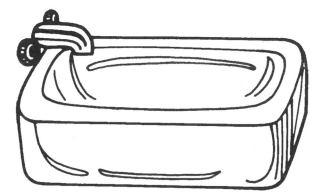

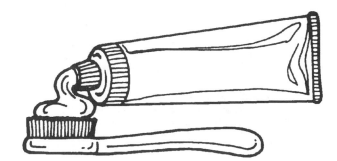

How Many Things In The House?

1. Count.
2. Print Numbers.
3. Color.

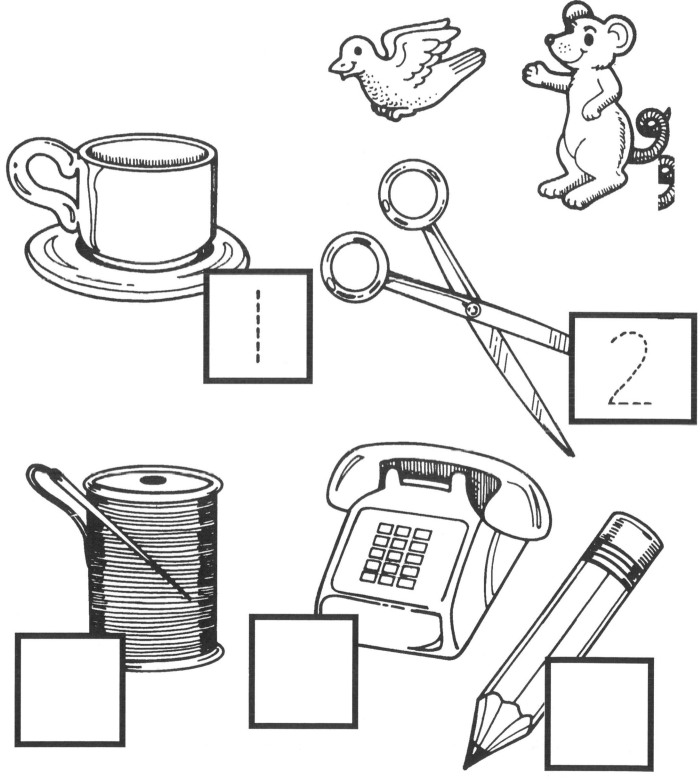

Your Bedroom

1. Draw some things in your bedroom.
2. Color the picture.

Name _____

In a House

Draw and color.

Draw 6 🍵 's. Color.

Draw 2 💡 's. Color.

Draw 3 🔑 's. Color.

Draw 5 🥄 's. Color.

House Pattern

* See suggested activity page 90.

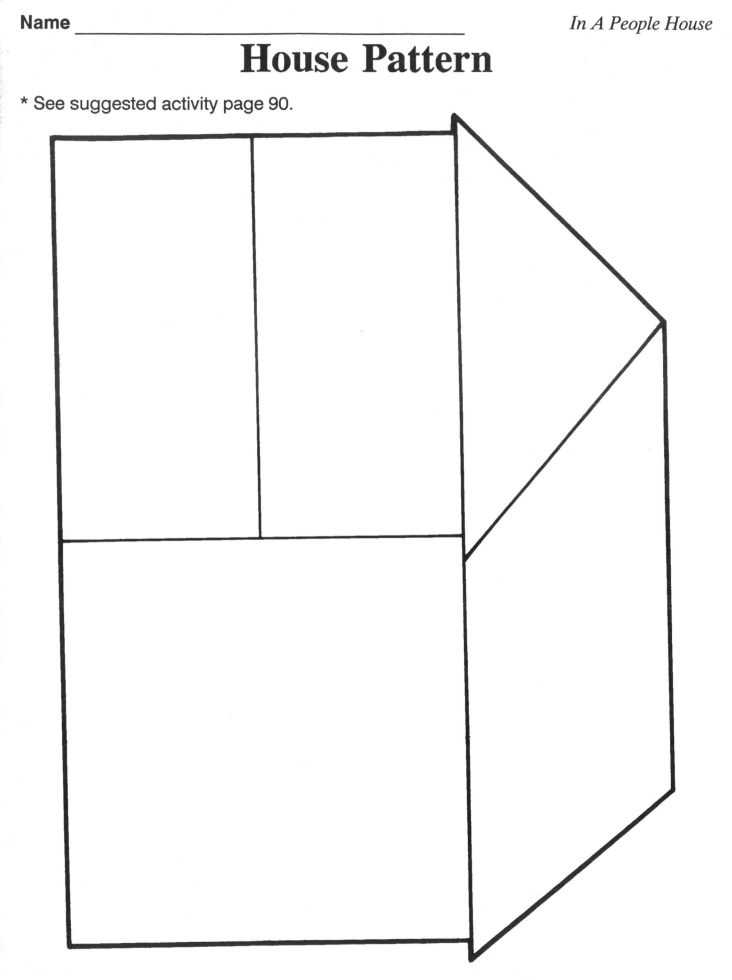